FAITH FUEL

A refueling journey

Tony Nolan

PRESS

Faith Fuel
A Refueling Journey
by Tony Nolan

Printed in the United States of America

ISBN 978-1-60266-841-6

www.xulonpress.com

Contents

Dedication

To my wife, Tammy, for really meaning it when you said, "I will." Your commitment to my usefulness in God's kingdom is why this book exists.

Acknowledgements

R elationships are the treasures that make life rich. I am grateful for the friends who have enriched this project. To the Casting Crowns band I want to say thanks for being the same both on and off stage. You inspire me. To our Assistant Brittany Brummel, you are a Godsend. Rachael Lovingood will forever be praised! Your tweaks and reordering of thoughts helped shape my first book and fuel the faith of a new generation. To Kerry Bural, I express unspeakable thankfulness for being a source of unending wisdom. To the team at Xulon Press, I extend a deep appreciation for your partnership with me in making this book materialize. And to our Lord Jesus I say most gratefully, thanks for taking the canvas of my life and painting a masterpiece of yourself to show the whole world how glorious you are!

Foreword

Tony Nolan has been a close family friend of mine for more than eight years. We met at a summer camp, and I immediately knew he was different. He had a passion for souls that didn't just live on the stage. He loved my students before he met them as though he could feel their hurt and knew only Jesus could restore them. I learned that God used his own life experience to shape his heart for others.

Tony grew up in a nightmarish world of abuse, abandonment, and bitterness toward a God he believed had put him there. God reached down into the pit of tragic choices he had dug for himself and placed him on the Rock of His Son. Tony never turned back to the life he had lived, but he never forgot the painful life he endured and poor choices he'd made. You can see in his eyes the love he has for the hurting, and you can hear in his voice the urgency of his message. In his book *Faith Fuel* Tony gives practical steps he uses every day in a "walking around friendship" with God. I pray your next thirty-one days bring you closer to Him and that your changed life will fuel the faith of those around you.

Love them like Jesus
Mark Hall
Casting Crowns

Introduction

My wife and I love to drive. Jump in the car, turn up the tunes, race along the road, and scope out some geography. Some of the best times I have had with Tammy have been during long drives. We cruise, talk, laugh, and just absorb each other. I call those moments our into-each-otherness.

One beautiful day in Dallas, Texas, we took off for a drive. Our car was a small three-cylinder trap called a Sprint. It was only a little bigger than a golf cart. Pulling up next to a semi-trailer truck on the interstate was always good for our prayer lives! Driving along the highway we were totally into each other when all of a sudden I noticed a flashing red light on the dashboard. I don't know much about cars, but I do know a blinking light on the instrument panel is not a good thing. I started feeling uneasy. A closer look at the intermittent glow confirmed my fear—the fuel gauge was on E!

Now I like to think of myself as a sensitive husband. I've attended several "be a better husband" conferences. So with all the compassion I could muster, I looked at my wife and said, "You bonehead! We are on E!"

She looked at me as if I were a total goober and said, "We have an extra fifteen or twenty miles in this tank."

I know you can get really great mileage out of a three-cylinder car, but "E" always means *empty,* not *extra!* All of our into-each-otherness dropped like a bad cell phone moment. Running on E is not good for your relationship.

Our spiritual journey is much like a road trip. We are cruising in the car of Christianity, sitting in the front seat with Jesus, and He calls the journey abundant life. Revving the engine of redemption, we shift through the gears of grace and navigate along the highway of God's will. We have the windows down and worship tunes blaring! As we race past those in the slow lane, they get a glimpse of the shoe-polish graffiti on our back window that says, "Enjoying Jesus!" Life is good, and we are into God.

The Bible tells us faith fuels this spiritual excursion. Romans 1:17 says, "The just *shall* live by faith" (italics added). That means having faith is not an option. As a combustible engine requires gasoline, so our lives require faith to move forward. And when you have it, faith is the fuel that propels us into extraordinary expeditions with God. The book of Hebrews says by *faith* Noah prepared an ark and salvaged mankind; by *faith* Abraham offered up Isaac; by *faith* Sarah conceived a child; by *faith* Moses led the people of God out of slavery; by *faith* the walls of Jericho fell! *Faith* fueled some astonishing accomplishments for God's glory. All of these heroes of the faith were faithful because they were faith-full. See it?

Most people I meet seem to be running on E spiritually. *I have totally been there too.* And I discovered that when our faith is depleted we don't enjoy Jesus; instead we endure the journey. There are no deep level conversations and there is no into-each-otherness. Our faithfulness turns into faithless-ness. But the crazy thing is, we keep the pedal to the floor and drive on. It seems as if life demands it. We have homework to finish, chores to do, part-time jobs to work, blogs to post, e-mails to return, and the list never seems to end. Be advised by a fellow traveler who has run out of gas and walked many a miserable mile: You may be able to overlook the alerting lights on your spiritual dashboard, but *you can't run on the fumes for long.* You need to make sure you have the stuff in your tank that will get you to God's daily destinations.

This book is a spiritual fueling station. It's all about getting some faith fuel so you can be faith-full to be faithful. Don't try to say that fast, or it will hurt your face. Just keep reading this book. After reading *Faith Fuel* over the next thirty-one days, you will find yourself like Stephen, who is described in Acts 6:8 as "full of faith."

Right now you might be thinking, *Wasn't he the guy who got stoned to death? Not sure I want to sign up for that. You should have used a different example, and then maybe I'd keep reading.* Be careful not to miss the point. He is a perfect spokesman for faith fuel. Yes, things got ugly for him, but that's part of the journey in a sin-cursed world. We will all have hard roads to travel. Stephen's life reveals that being full of faith helps us live in such a way that no matter what trials come along we can reach our ultimate destination, giving God glory! *Faith Fuel* will help you get faith-full, and you'll be faithful!

Chapter 1

Fueling Guide

E ach daily experience is laid out like a stop at QuickTrip, a major fueling station and convenience store that is taking over the entire known world. The first thing you do at a gas station is position your car to receive the fuel. It never fails—I always pull up on the wrong side of the pump. *Faith Fuel positions you to refuel.* *Faith Fuel* consists of thirty-one daily devotions that contain three sequential refueling experiences. Let me walk you through each of these moments.

The first is a GET IT moment.

GET IT

After you position yourself at the pump, then you fill 'er up! With the hose in, click the little "make it stay in place thingy" and pour in the combustible fluid. Each *Faith Fuel* devotion begins with a unique story, word picture, or experience that helps you pour in some faith.

Then there is the CAP IT moment.

CAP IT

Have you seen people drive off without putting the gas cap back on? With the cost of gas nowadays, it is a sad sight to see someone drive off and spew fuel all over the road. The same goes for your time in this book. You need to make sure that what gets in *stays in*. The devotion includes a CAP IT moment. It consists of a couple of questions that serve as a link to help you download the core elements of the GET IT moment.

Finally there is the USE IT moment.

USE IT

What a waste if you get fuel and keep it, but it does not take you anywhere! At the close of each chapter, you will be challenged to use the fuel you received. I will encourage you with several engaging and practical steps that will propel you forward in the incredible journey of faith. Hebrews 11:1 says, "Faith is the substance of things hoped for, the *evidence* of things not seen." In just thirty-one short days you will have an incredible collage of memories outlining and underscoring the validity of your faith in the living God, Jesus Christ our Lord.

Are you ready to ride? I'll drive, and you ride shotgun. So let's go!

Chapter 2

Spiritual Ketchup

GET IT

My kids love candy, but they hate to eat healthy food. They actually can't swallow it. I thought they were going to shrivel up and die. Really, they didn't eat and started looking like the children people adopt from third-world countries.

I prayed, God answered, and all I can say is, "Praise God for ketchup!" It is the only power that can open the tightly clinched jaws of my kids! They love the stuff! I can get them to eat anything as long as it is covered with the awesome red sauce. Now they eat all kinds of foods and are stronger and healthier. Sometimes the Bible is hard to swallow. It has so much variety to offer, but lots of people only nibble on a couple of the sweet promises and refuse to have a balanced, healthy diet. This results in loss of strength and emotional instability, which is really spiritual malnourishment.

I have been in that pitiful, powerless position of not being able to take the meaty stuff of the Word of God. I was shriveling up spiritually and taking in an unbalanced diet until I discovered what I call "spiritual ketchup." This ketchup is really a series of questions you can use to guide your Bible reading and help you swallow and digest the Word of God.

I have listed these questions here for you to use. Go ahead. Try it. I'm sure you'll like it. Bon appétit!

1. **Is there an insight?** Watch for insights in the Scriptures that can help you know God better or show you something about who He is and what His character is. We know God through His Word. As you read, keep this question in mind. As you discover things about God, praise Him for who He is and live in light of it.

2. **Is there a principle?** Principles are truths that provide power for living. The Bible contains a lot of them. Note them and let them rule your decisions.

3. **Is there a command?** God's Word is filled with commands, things He has told us to do. As you read find out what they are and obey God. Remember that God blesses us according to our obedience, and partial obedience is not obedience.

4. **Is there a prohibition?** God has also told us some things not to do. These are referred to as "prohibitions." Underline and adhere to the "do nots" in Scripture. Recall again that God's blessings are a product of our obedience.

5. **Is there a promise?** Some things God has said He will do in our lives. I have found that marking these in the Word and depositing them in the bank of my heart provides me with great spiritual wealth. Claim the promises; they are ours for the taking if our motives are to live for the Lord's glory and the advancement of His kingdom.

6. **Is there a special word?** At times you may be going through something in your life, and a Scripture verse or phrase will "jump out of the Bible and into your soul." I call these special words. It's almost as if you're online with heaven when you're reading, and then you hear, "You've got mail!" God e-mails your heart. Write these words down, inhale them in your spiritual lungs, and

be refreshed: *God has not forgotten you, and He is in control!*

CAP IT

1. Fill in the answers: "Principles are _____ that provide _____ for living."
2. What is a prohibition?
3. What must our motives be in order for us to claim God's promises?

USE IT

1. Go to www.tonynolan.org and click on my journal page. Scroll through the archives and find Spiritual Ketchup. Highlight it and print it out. Place it in your Bible.
2. Begin reading through your Bible every day. Several plans are out there to follow and read your Bible in a year. Visit www.studylight.org and you will find a great one.
3. As you read, keep this guide handy and use it to get all the fuel you can because faith comes by hearing the Word of God.

Chapter 3

Miraculous Merge

GET IT

I have the privilege of being involved in the Christian music industry. I pastor artists, and I get to preach at their concerts. My behind-the-scenes access has provided many spiritual moments that have fueled my faith by the gallons. I will be sharing several of these candid moments with you throughout this book. I hope the perspectives help to open your spiritual reservoir and flood it. The following is one of those moments.

I just got out of catering. It's the place most artists go to get semi-nourishment and a full stomach. I'm taking an unexpected trip to the restroom (there is a connection), then I'm headed for the stage.

The hallway leading to the stage is vibrating from a kick pedal and a hyper drummer. I am fully vib'n with the music as I peer through the curtain to take a look at the crowd. It's a full house. My eyes go straight toward a girl in the floor seats. She's a teenager, sporting black boots with cut-off jean shorts, a skater tank top, and more gaudy bracelets than the wife of King Tut. Her disposition seems to lean a bit toward the axe murderer side. I'm not being judgmental; I'm just making an observation. She is sitting with her arms folded across her chest. She has a bothered look that says, "Don't even try to reach me; I'm totally not into God." I look around at the masses, and it appears she has brought a posse of like-minded skeptics. I see her heart mirrored in the eyes of countless others. I cry. Not just tears, but a deep agonizing cry because I know where they are. I lived on that same street in a pain-filled pad at the bottom of Hurting Hill.

At first I am tempted to let her have her way. I don't want to upset anyone—just kindly back away and let her stay in her condo of criticism. All of a sudden the lights flash and brilliantly accent the stage with wild blues and intense deep purples. There is an explosion, and the arena is saturated in a flurry of voices (more like a roar) and music. A whole different vibe rises from the seats, and it's contagious.

Something phenomenal is happening. All the cynics are subdued and awestruck by the power of praise. Locked hearts fling open as the keyboard, drums, bass, and guitar work like a Special Forces agent rescuing hostages from their cells. The band through their lyrics invites them to escape their prison and run with them to a better place.

The music fades, and I am now center stage. It's my honor to partner with the music artist and share the good news of the gospel. I watch with dropped jaw and fluttering heart as scores of the "don't ever try to reach me" crowd begin to flood forward in response to the gospel invitation. Like dolphins that have been freed from the captor's net, they are dancing and jumping for joy. The audience thunders with applause, welcoming their new brothers and sisters into the family. As I join in the clapping, I am ambushed at the thought of millions of angels cheering even louder at the same moment in heaven!

I exit stage left and answer the gesture of oncoming band members with a loud slapping high five. Walking behind the stage I take a moment to kneel and thank the Lord for His faithfulness and love. Before I head to my dressing room,

I take another peek at the crowd from behind the curtain. There she is again. The now-reached, don't-reach-me girl, and her face is drenched with tears. She is crying and smiling both. The girl standing next to her is crying more than she is. I find out later the second girl's weeping was in response to seeing her prayers answered. Her friend did not know Christ, so she brought her to the concert with high hopes. Now she'll go home with an answered prayer and a best-friend-turned-sister story to tell. The backstage hall is now filled with melodious harmony, intermingled with words of praise. God is good, I think. Tonight music and ministry merged, and the result was nothing short of a miracle.

CAP IT

1. What was the lost girl's attitude about me before she got saved? Hint: "Don't even . . ."
2. What did her friend do that turned her into a "sister"?
3. What phenomena subdued the cynics?

USE IT

1. Add Christian concerts to your daily prayer list. Pray that God will use every concert to open the hearts of the lost to His great salvation.
2. Find out when and where your favorite Christian band is doing a concert. Buy two tickets, one for you and one for someone who needs the Jesus the band will be singing about.
3. Start a prayer ministry for your music ministry at your church. Get other people to join you and pray before the service that God would use it to help people find a "better" place.

Chapter 4

Crown Your Prayer Time

GET IT

Thousands were saved at a tour I did with Casting Crowns; the tour was called *Lifesong*. One of my passions is to make sure those who get saved also get started. Get started on the right foot in prayer, that is. So I developed a simple-to-follow prayer guide for them to track with during their prayer time. It doesn't matter if you just received Jesus or are a seasoned saint, this guide will lend you insights into prayer—and prayer fuels your faith.

Follow this simple plan to accent your prayer time with God. Take time every morning and find a quiet place. Close out distractions and fix your mind on God. Let this acrostic (c.r.o.w.n.s.) serve as a prayer point guide.

C–Commit your time to God by saying something like, "Dear God, here I am. I desire to be with You. I have things on my heart I want to talk to You about. My heart is open to hearing what You want to speak to me about." Then. . . .

R–Read some psalms to God. Just go though the book of Psalms and find one that resonates with your heart and read it out loud! He delights in hearing His children praise Him and adore Him through what has been declared about Him in His Word. Then. . . .

O–Open your mind to the voice of truth and close out all negative thoughts from the enemy, Satan. Just read out loud what His Word says about Him; now read out loud what His Word says about you! Start today by reading Romans chapter 8 out loud. Do it now. Read it again slowly. See it? Yes, you are loved and always will be, no matter what. Now. . . .

W–Write out the things that are on your heart. Sins you are dealing with. Struggles you are facing at school and in your life. Things you need or desire to see happen. Write them out, then go through the list and talk to God about them. Ask Him for help. After you do, read Hebrews 4:16. Feast your eyes on that spiritual buffet again, and this time read it more slowly. He will help you in your time of need. Then. . . .

N–Never be guilty of not asking because you think your requests are insignificant to God. He says in 1 Peter 5:7, "casting all your cares upon Him, for he cares for you." And in James 4:2 we read, "You do not have because you do not ask."

S–Surrender your request to His will. Matthew 6:33 says, "But seek first the kingdom of God, and His righteousness, and all these things will be added to you." What is that all about? It means that as we surrender all of our wants, desires, and ambitions so that God's will can be accomplished for His glory and the advancement of His kingdom, then He's got our back! He will take care of you and answer your prayers, maybe not when or how we want, but He does answer.

Little extra: Go to www.tonynolan.org and visit our resource page. I have an MP3 message on prayer called "He Can Hear You Now." It's a must-hear, and it will enhance your prayer life. Go pray!

CAP IT

1. To start your prayer time, you need to _____ your time to God.
2. What verse is called a spiritual buffet in the W part of the acrostic?

USE IT

1. Start today and pray. Set aside thirty minutes every morning and pray by following along with this guide.
2. Find and write out Hebrews 4:16. Place it next to the area where you sleep. Read it before you go to bed and first thing when you wake up. Let it drive you to His throne.

Chapter 5

A Mark Moment

GET IT

Some of my best friends in the world are the band members in the contemporary Christian music group Casting Crowns. Millions of people enjoy their music. Because of the relationship I've shared with them over eight years, I get to enjoy some spiritually invigorating moments. With their permission I will be sharing things about them that have fueled my faith. You will find them sprinkled throughout this book. Today I want to share a very special moment that I had with lead singer Mark Hall.

On September 29, 2005, Mark gave me a devotional book we would be going through together on our concert tour. He had given it to me the night before. As I opened it, I noticed that he had written a note to me in the flyleaf. It read:

TONY! It's taken some time, but we are running side-by-side in ministry. Thank you for your friendship and for being a part of this!

Love them like Jesus!
Mark Hall

I closed the book and smiled. It's great to serve the Lord with a friend.

It's morning, and I'm on the Halls' family bus headed toward our next concert to serve, as he said, "side-by-side." Waking up on a bus is hard. No, after an evening of trying to sleep as we bounced all over the highway, it's impossible. Mark is seated across from me, and we're trying to shake off the sleep monster luring us back to our bunks. We both take a look out the bus window. There it is again, the blurry outside miles passing under us as we race toward another opportunity to make great the name of God!

He smiles at me and asks, "Sleep well?"

I nod and offer a half-awake "Did fine," which translates, "Oh, no! When will I ever get some real sleep?"

Mark says, "Me too."

Breakfast bowls start flying out, and we dish up the Lucky Charms. Four spoons full and the sugar rush begins. With the sleep monster on the run we are grinning from ear to ear, agreeing these little "yummies" will be served at the marriage supper of the Lamb. Our morning talk begins.

"Did you read the e-mails I sent you?" Mark asks.

"No," I reply. "I can't get them in this area. No signal."

"Let me tell you about them," he says. If you've ever had the opportunity to listen to Mark as he talks about God's great power to help people in a time of need, then you know he radiates joy.

He laughs and says, "God is so cool. In the past week I have received several e-mails telling me how God has done miracles. One family had a dad who was abusive to his wife and children. After listening to "American Dream" he fell in repentance and is now treating them right and getting into God. A mom and dad wrote and said that even though their baby girl is dying of cancer they have joy knowing where she is going. God is giving them strength. A teenager wrote and was cutting. She was really messed up. But through our ministry God touched her life. She is no longer the dark cutter kid. She is full of life and is being used by God to help other cutters stop the bleeding!"

We threw out a high five, which is a totally nutty thing to do but a must for very cool men. Our eyes gazed out the bus windows again.

While watching the telephone lines go up and down with every fifty feet of highway, I reflected. I was keenly aware of something going on inside of me and felt a power surge. My inner spirit was stirred, and I felt strongly affirmed in my faith. Psalm 9:9–10 is true: "The Lord also will be a refuge for the oppressed, a refuge in times of trouble. . .for You, Lord, have not forsaken those who seek You." God is alive, and He is at work. Faith is not simply dreaming and wishing for God-things to happen. His power is evident in lives that have been altered by His love, mercy, and power. Don't let go of the nozzle on this one. Let's squeeze in on this truth.

CAP IT

1. I started this devotion by sharing with you the note Mark wrote. What did he say we were doing side-by-side?
2. Faith is not simply _____ and _____ for God-things to happen.
3. What supports the evidence that God's power alters lives?

USE IT

1. Find a friend today and make a creed to serve side-by-side in ministry together.
2. Pick a day out of the week and meet with each other and talk about what God is doing.
3. Start a journal and write down the stories you hear of how God changed a life. Go to it from time to time so

you see God's track record and build up your faith to trust Him.

Chapter 6

Clarity

GET IT

I am one of those guys who doesn't get it right off the bat. I need things to be clarified. I am so bad at "not getting it" that I think my spiritual gift is asking, "Huh?"

I heard a story about a young man who needed a little clarification concerning a traffic violation he committed. He was driving and came to a stop sign. Instead of stopping, he did a little bump and roll, only slowing down slightly.

Well, the policeman pulled him over. "Give me your driver's license and registration, please."

"I didn't do anything wrong," the boy said.

"Yes, you did," said the policeman. "Now give me your driver's license, please."

"No, sir, I did not do anything wrong," repeated the boy.

"Yes, you did. You didn't stop at the sign. You just slowed down."

"I most certainly did stop."

"No, you did not. Now give me your driver's license!"

Then, with a great attitude, the boy declared, "I will not give you my driver's license until you can tell me the difference between what you call a stop and what I call a stop!"

Immediately the policeman yanked that boy out of his car. He started beating him with his maximum kick'-em night stick. "I've got a question for you, boy," he said. "Do you want me to stop, or do you want me to slow down?"

I believe he clarified it.

I am so glad that when a mixed-up, confused world needed some clarity about their sins, God chose not to beat us with a stick. Instead He loved us with a cross! And through the cross God *clears up* an amazing reality—John 8:32. "And you shall know the truth, and the truth shall make you free!" Truth is a person, and His name is Jesus. But truth is also found in principles that come from the person. One of the biggest truths that can set you free is the truth about you. Absorb this thought: *What's true about you is what God says about you.* Read that last statement again. Now say it again out loud.

John 10:10 says the thief comes to steal, kill, and destroy. One of the devil's most terrorizing tactics is to make sure you don't get set free with that truth. He wants to hold you hostage and get you to believe that what your past says about you, what your present problems say about you, and what those little voices in your head say about you is what's true about you. As a result thousands of people commit suicide every year because they have been robbed of their "God value."

Jesus releases you from the mental and emotional bondage the devil puts on you and frees you to live, really live. Christians are "loved, favored and accepted". The Bible says in Ephesians 2:10 that you are His "workmanship." That word means *work of art.* You are a unique work of art God has brought into this world for His purposes. *Your life is a canvas on which God wants to paint a masterpiece to show the whole world just how glorious He is!* It's time to refuse to listen to the lies from the enemy. Jesus clarified the issue on the cross—live in your freedom.

CAP IT

1. What is one of the devil's most terrorizing tactics?
2. What's true about you is what _____ says about you.
3. God says you are _____, _____, and _____!

USE IT

1. Take a small piece of paper and write the following letters on it: WTAYIWGSAY. It looks a little crazy, I know, but each letter is the first letter of the words in the phrase "What's true about you is what God says about you."
2. Now tape that paper to a prominent place in your car or in your room. Seeing it there will remind you of its truth and will help you choose to leave the prison of lies and live in the truth of God's Word. You are who He says you are.

Chapter 7

WD-40 for the Mind

GET IT

I love music, and I especially love Christian music. The truth is that music is a tool Christians can use to connect with the Spirit of God and find power to live for God's glory. Ephesians 5:18 resonates with this principle. The apostle Paul challenged us to be filled with the Spirit of God, singing songs and hymns and spiritual songs.

Think about it this way: Christian songs are WD-40 for the mind. For those who are not in the know about WD-40, please allow me the honor of introducing you to this miracle fluid. It's a little spray oil that really works! I'm talking hoist the Titanic engines up from the ocean floor, spray a little WD-40 on the rusted parts, and va-vroom! It would start. Okay, maybe an exaggeration, but for those of you who have seen this stuff in action you know it's a possibility.

Now I'll say it again. Christian music is WD-40 for the mind. A good soaking under anointed music will have you rust-free and thinking clearly!

Our brains are really cool. I was watching a Discovery Channel show once, and it told all kinds of awesome things our minds can do. It can handle up to ten thousand decisions per second, detect infinitely small tastes, and smell more than ten million different odors. I know this last fact to be true because I have done a ton of youth camps, and a middle-school student who has skipped his bath for a week can test the limits of our smelling abilities. Our brains are amazing.

The problem is, our minds get flooded with the ideas and influences of our Christ-less culture, clogging and smothering our mental gears till they lock up. Like the rusting skeleton of the once great Titanic, we become mentally lifeless as the currents of our culture rip through the fabric of our minds and slowly decay our ability to think clearly about God. I've been there, and it's a sad and scary place to live.

A good remedy for this condition is to soak daily in some solid Christian songs. Expose your mind to the faith-firming lyrics of David Crowder who declares, "Here is our God who has come to bring us back to Him." Focus on the clarification Nichole Nordeman gives as she sings about Jesus. "You came to take us and to wake us up to something more than we always settle for." Soar heavenward with Chris Tomlin and shout, "You are amazing, God!" Awaken as Mark Hall passionately declares the power of our identity in Christ and says, "I AM YOURS!" Listen and all of a sudden you feel it. The lyrics soak in, and the rust begins to loosen its grip—it feels good to be free. Free to feed on truth, to understand our identity, to embrace faith and worship God authentically.

CAP IT
1. The currents of our culture slowly decay our ability to think _____ about _____.
2. What can Christian music do for our minds?

USE IT
1. Take twenty minutes this morning and listen to some of your favorite Christian music artists during your devotional time. Some of my favorites are Casting

Crowns, Will Goodwin, Jackson Waters, and Sanctus Real.

2. Write on paper one of the lines in the song that jumps out at you. Stick it in your Bible, and reference it now and again. You may even want to go listen to it again.

3. Read Ephesians 5:18–19. What role does it say music has in helping you connect with the Spirit of God?

Chapter 8

Clean for Our King

GET IT

In the Old Testament we find an interesting practice. Leviticus reveals the bathing procedure of any person preparing to be in the presence of God. Read the whole book, and you will find the bath was much more than a quick slip into a cold, low-water-pressure, locker-room shower or the occasional sink bath. *I remember those too well while on tour.* They had to do some serious cleaning before they could even approach holy God.

Now through the new covenant we can approach God through the cleanliness of Jesus. This is good news. We do not have to do all the obligated bathing in order to be in the presence of God. But, even though we don't have to, perhaps we should.

For our appointed daily eating times, we don't have to wash our hands, but it is better for us if we do. For our date nights with our special someone, we don't have to get dressed up to go out. But, oh, the delightful twinkle in their surprised eyes when we do! *It most definitely is better!*

Now transfer that whole "don't have to but better if you do" thing over to our approaching face-to-face moment with our heavenly king. Oh, how much better is it to be clean for our king? Think of the smile we will spread across the face of divinity because of our preparation for His presence.

I was in a Church service one day and heard a preacher quote Spurgeon, "Let's not let the fingers that will cast our crowns be tarnished with the filth of flesh! Our feet soon will skip across the paths paved gold in the land fairer than day; therefore keep them free of the soil of selfishness. May our minds not be soaked with sinfulness so we can fully absorb the out pouring of heaven's glory. Let our eyes reveal no reflection of sights unholy when they peer deep into the eyes of God." Oh, how much better will it be when we are clean for our king!

Now read again a text message keyed by the Holy Spirit of God. James 1:27 says, "Pure and undefiled religion before God and the Father is this: to visit orphans and widows in their trouble, and *to keep oneself unspotted from the world*" (italics added). Keep it clean for our king!

CAP IT
1. In the Old Testament what did someone have to do before approaching God?
2. Now through the _____ of Jesus we _____ _____ God!
3. We don't _____ to get clean, but it would be _____ if we did.

USE IT
1. List four ways you can stay clean and "unspotted" from this world.
2. Go buy a small bar of soap. Don't open it. Just write the word *KING* on it with a permanent pen. Place that bar in a spot where you may need a reminder to be clean, like by a computer or on top of the TV set. Just put it there for you to see and, in doing so, let it remind you to keep it clean for the king!

Chapter 9

The Fro-Hawk is fro-real!

GET IT

I often wear my hair in a fro-hawk. That's when you push it all forward and have it sticking up in the middle but only in the front and on top of your head. Little children have told me I look like a chicken. They are so brutal but so honest.

Chris Huffman is the inspiration for my hair. No, Chris is not a chicken (only when it comes to dancing on the stage). Chris is the bass player for Casting Crowns. He has really cool hair. As a preconcert ritual, Chris takes some Got2 Be Glued hair gel and spikes his hair all up in the front, on the top, and in the back, to look like a Mohawk. But the sides are not shaved so it is called a fro-hawk. Most people who have this hair carry a crazy punker persona.

You would think the fro-hawk dude would be a head-banging wild man. Actually his demeanor really does not fit his hair. Chris is usually a very quiet and mild person. There is nothing "punky" about him. Most punk people I meet want you to walk away understanding how cool and great they are. Chris is the kind of guy you can sit down with and no positioning happens. He is your equal, and when you walk away he makes you feel better about yourself.

More than having cool hair, Chris cares. He is a very caring brother. Some things went wrong with my health, and he gave me a call. WOW! I got a call from the bass player of Casting Crowns. And if you think I got jazzed about that, then you should have seen my boy's face when Chris called him to wish him a happy birthday when he turned seven. *Chris cares.* Someone once told me you can tell how real a person is by how much they care. My kids will be in the bath and lather their heads with shampoo, spike up their hair, and scream, "I want to be like Chris!" Inside my heart I say, *I sure hope so because the world needs more people who are real.*

CAP IT
1. What is the one thing I highlighted about Chris that makes him real?
2. When you walk away, Chris makes you feel better about _____.
3. Do you think the world needs more people who are real? Why?

USE IT
1. Make a list of the people you consider to be real.
2. Take a moment and identify the things that make them so authentic.
3. Pick the top two traits that make them genuine and ask someone to hold you accountable to develop them in your own life.

Chapter 10

Witness Worship

GET IT

Have you ever felt as if something was missing from your worship? As I cross the country, there is a buzz about the void that exists in the present worship movement. People are looking for something more than just singing about God in a service. They sense deep inside that another element of worship can be experienced. They are right, because Jesus is calling us to a deeper level of worship. It's called witness worship.

In Matthew 4:19 you can see how Jesus called some of the first disciples. "Follow Me, and I will make you fishers of men." When Jesus called those first disciples, He was calling them to more than they were at the time. He was inviting them into a relationship with Him through which they would be transformed into fishers of men. You have also been called to that same relationship, and He wants to transform you just as He did the disciples.

Jesus calls His worshippers to be fishers of men. Our worship must transcend our services and show up in our witnessing to others about Christ. That means witnessing is worship! Every true worshipper will never be fully satisfied with just telling God He is great; they must also tell of His greatness to others. It's a call for us to move beyond merely considering what Jesus would do and start copying what He did. He worshipped the Father by telling the lost about His salvation.

Throughout my travels in recent days, I've been excited to see thousands of "witness worshippers" tracking with this call of God. They worship God by inviting others to become worshippers of Jesus! They are willing to live in such a way that God tosses them into the ocean of this sin-cursed world where the lost see them and are drawn toward God and then get hooked up with Jesus! Few things will fuel your faith like sharing your faith. The bottom line is, *your worship has something missing if your worship isn't fishing.*

CAP IT
1. What is the current buzz about in the modern worship movement?
2. The deeper level of worship is called _____.
3. A witness worshipper lives in such a way that God _____.

USE IT
1. Get a sheet of paper and write down the names of people you know who are not connected with Jesus.
2. Begin adding them to your daily prayer time.

Chapter 11

Fishing Tips

GET IT

As I travel across the country, I have the privilege of ministering alongside some cool Christians like Rebecca St. James, Jeremy Camp, Mac Powell, and Mark Hall. They are all fishers of men, and they passionately agree that *our worship has something missing if our worship isn't fishing.* Watching them and noting other true worshippers, I hacked in and broke the code on what propels people to worship though their witness. These things are biblically sound and are the same reasons why I love to be a fanatical fisher of men! These thoughts will inspire you to worship through your witness.

1. Because of what it does for God's smile!

Hebrews 13:15–16 says, "Therefore by Him let us continually offer the sacrifice of praise that is, the fruit of our lips, giving thanks to His name. But do not forget to do good and to share, for with such sacrifices God is well pleased." It pleases the heart of God when we share Jesus!

I wear a medical bracelet. It is a tool I developed to help me be a witness worshipper. A lot of people look at me as if I'm some right-wing "Jesus freak." Some snarl and ask,

"You believe that—that there's only one way to heaven, that Jesus is God and He rose from the dead? You're an idiot." They reject me and bash me. I don't like that. I want to be accepted. My flesh wants to back off and say, "I was just kidding." I don't want them mad and rejecting me.

But I remember Hebrews 13:15. And it empowers me to be bold. I am instantly encouraged, knowing my worship has pleased the heart of God. The whole world may attack and reject us, but what a thought it is to know God is in heaven calling out to His angelic hosts: "That's My child!" We should share because of what it does for the smile of God!

2. Because of what it does for our spirits!

Luke 15:6–7 says, "...rejoice with me, for I have found my lost sheep. I say to you that likewise there will be more joy in heaven over *one* sinner who repents than over ninety-nine just persons who need no repentance." Do you ever get bored with church? You go, but it's the same ole la-dee-da. Go "men fishing," and it will fire you up!

One summer I fished a tournament with my father-in-law and five-year-old-son, Wil. We started out great. Buck got one on his line and gave the pole to Wil. That fish was about four pounds! Great catch! But for the rest of the day, we did not catch a thing. No bites, nothing—just bobbing up and down in the blazing heat till the mayonnaise on our sandwiches turned into a clear jelly. It was awful. At the end of the day, we could hear the other fishermen asking each other how many they had caught. We heard the big numbers they shouted: "15!" "22!" and so on. Then they looked at us. We were silenced. We couldn't compete with that, we thought. At that moment my five-year-old, Wil, stood straight up on the bow of the boat and cheerfully hollered, "One!" We were embarrassed but he was thrilled over catching just one.

In like manner it does something for our spirits when we see one of our friends or family members give their lives to

Jesus. We join a spiritual party in heaven rejoicing over just one.

3. Because of what it does for their souls!

In 2 Peter 3:3–4, 7–12, we read, "…knowing this first: that scoffers will come in the last days, walking according to their own lusts, and saying, "Where is the promise of His coming? For since the fathers fell asleep, all things continue as *they were* from the beginning of creation." "…But the heavens and the earth *which* are now preserved by the same word, are reserved for fire until the day of judgment and perdition of ungodly men. But, beloved, do not forget this one thing, that with the Lord one day *is* as a thousand years, and a thousand years as one day. The Lord is not slack concerning *His* promise, as some count slackness, but is longsuffering toward us, not willing that any should perish but that all should come to repentance. But the day of the Lord will come as a thief in the night, in which the heavens will pass away with a great noise, and the elements will melt with fervent heat; both the earth and the works that are in it will be burned up. Therefore, since all these things will be dissolved, what manner *of persons* ought you to be in holy conduct and godliness, looking for and hastening the coming of the day of God, because of which the heavens will be dissolved, being on fire, and the elements will melt with fervent heat?

John 3:16 says, "For God so loved the world that He gave His only begotten Son, that whosoever believes in Him should not perish but have everlasting life." We must keep fishing. We must engage in witness worship so others won't suffer the coming wrath of God and perish but have everlasting life. Don't you want to see people make heaven and miss hell?

September 11, 2001, was tragic. It is hard to erase the mental images of fireballs, crumbled buildings, and people jumping to their deaths. What a horrible day! Did you know there were some people who were under investigation for allegedly knowing about the terrorist plot? That's right. CNN reported that fifteen hundred people did not show up for work that day, and the FBI was informed these people did so because they knew it was going to happen.

Let me ask you a question. What if they did know? Would you agree with me that if they did know and saved their own lives, they also had a moral obligation to save others? Yes! Everyone agrees they were morally obligated. Well, the investigation concluded that they did not know about the coming attacks. So they were off the hook.

But we do know of a certain day. It will be a day no one has ever seen before. What we just read from the Bible tells us it will be a terrible day when God will pour out His wrath. But be sure it will not be an act of terrorism. Rather it will be a *holy act of justice*. We know this day is coming, and many of us have positioned ourselves to be saved. Good thing to do. But in the name of Jesus, don't you see that this call to worship through our witness is a matter of eternal spiritual obligation? We should not just make sure we are going to be okay on that day but that others will be as well. We need to help them to be saved from the coming wrath of God and captured by His unfailing love.

CAP IT

1. Read Hebrews 13:15. God is well pleased when we do what?
2. According to Luke 15:6–7, heaven throws a slamming party over how many sinners who repent? Briefly describe how you felt when you were used by God in an act of worship that led someone to Christ.
3. Your worship has something _____ if your worship isn't _____!

USE IT

1. Go today and share Jesus with the people you have been praying for. Call them or take them to lunch. God will go with you!
2. Visit www.tonynolan.org and link up with my resource page. You will find a message called *Lifelift* there. Purchase it! It contains a great, easy, and fun way to share your faith. And be sure to get some witnessing bracelets with it. Thousands have been saved using the Lifelift tools. All the money we earn from the sales is deposited into our nonprofit organization and is used to underwrite our Lifelift Conferences so people can come to them free!

Chapter 12

Joining in the Warning

GET IT

What do those four words "joining in the warning" mean? People are seeing them on our website, reading them in blogs, and hearing them across the nation. What is "joining in the warning"?

God is using Casting Crowns to awaken the sleeping giant, the church, with their songs, but not everybody wants to get out of bed. Many critics complain that Casting Crowns' songs are too in-your-face. These people have missed it. No one is trying to get in someone's face, but they do want God to get in our hearts! This same slumbering crowd has attacked the message I preached at the Lifesong concert. Their assaults and apathy birthed the "joining in the warning" movement.

First, let me say I am always open to insights from others who criticize my ministry in an effort to help me. Proverbs 25:12, in *The Message,* says, "A wise friend's timely reprimand is like a gold ring slipped on your finger." I treasure such rebukes. They fuel growth. But there are some whose rebukes are not meant to help, but to hurt. Hurt me? God said I should expect it, but I cannot and will not let them hurt others and harm the kingdom of God! An e-mail that was sent from a "church-going Christian" is an example of what I am talking about. (Keep in mind I preached a twenty-minute message in which one minute and fifteen seconds was given to the subject this man blasts me about, and the remaining eighteen minutes and forty-five seconds were focused on the love and mercy of God.)

An anonymous person wrote, ". . . In our pluralistic and tolerant culture, it is totally inappropriate for someone to talk about death, judgment, and hell. This is manipulation and is in no way a representation of a voice of truth. . . ."

I replied to his mail. After mentioning the timescale of the message I stated earlier, I then wrote, ". . . As it relates to me mentioning hell and your suggestion that it is inappropriate, here is a thought. Suppose a volcano erupts in Hawaii. The lava flows under an overpass and knocks out a section of the bridge. *Unaware vacation travelers* are speeding toward the overpass and are in certain danger. Bystanders watch as *one man nearby passionately warns the travelers to stop and turn around.* The safe bystanders send him text messages *criticizing his efforts!* Here is a question to consider. Is it best for the bystanders to just keep critiquing his efforts or to begin *joining in the warning?* It's just a thought."

See it? Joining in the warning is a *response.* It was the heartfelt loving response of a *daring* and *caring* person. Daring? Yes! To interrupt the journey of the vacationing people, to leave the bystander support group and risk having those people turn into enemies and critics is not for the insecure. It's a response. It's also my response to what I see many bystanders in the church doing to the hell-bound travelers of this world.

I don't have to try hard to make a connection between the lava story and the truth found in the book of Revelation about God's coming judgment. As I have traveled across this nation, God has placed a raging fire in my bones—to snap out of my own bystander stare and break out an urgent call for others to risk caring enough to begin *joining in the warning!*

CAP IT

1 Do you think the bystanders should join in the warning? Why?
2. Which person in the story would you say cares the most?
3. Define in your own words what "joining in the warning" means to you.

USE IT

1. What risks will you have to take to leave the byway and get in the highway?
2. List the risks and ask God to give you grace to take them.
3. Do you hear the Spirit's witness to this call? Does it resonate in your innermost being? I want to hear your heart about this. E-mail your feedback to me personally at tony@tonynolan.org.

Chapter 13

Bloom Where You Are Planted

GET IT

I affectionately call Megan Garret "mega lungs." The girl can sing! She was not with Casting Crowns when I first met them down in Daytona. She merged into the family after they arrived at Eagles' Landing Baptist Church in Georgia.

I will never forget the first time I heard Megan sing. I leaned over and whispered in Mark Hall's ear, "Where did you find her?"

"God just dropped her in from heaven," he replied.

She is totally sent from God. On the tour Megan would always contribute to our devotional time by expressing some of the sweetest, most insightful thoughts. It did not take long for me to develop a deep respect for her talent and her testimony.

Let me tell you briefly how she got connected with Casting Crowns. She was leading worship for her youth group at Eagles' Landing Baptist Church. A dismaying event happened when the leader of the youth group left the church. When he departed a lot of Megan's friends took off as well. They begged her to go with them. But, as Megan recalls, "I just had this *conviction* that God did not call me to follow my friends but to serve Him faithfully." She stayed there singing her heart out leading a little group of students. It was tough. Many times she felt so lonely and missed her friends deeply. But she knew God had told her to stay. She chose to bloom where she was planted. God put her there, and she was going to grow and magnify Him there.

Then one day the church called a new youth leader to come and serve. His name was Mark Hall. Mark began to lead, and one of the biggest areas he wanted to get into right away was the worship time. He sat in on one of their youth services and heard the strong yet celestial vocal modulations of Megan Garret. In no time she was an official member of the Casting Crowns family.

Megan's story is like that of David, the little shepherd boy. *Serve where God plants you, and God will promote you.* Megan is an inspiration for me to serve God whole-heartedly in everything I do. Faith is living in the present with the future securely in God's hands.

CAP IT
1. What event caused Megan's friends to leave?
2. Megan recalled that God told her not to _____ her friends but to _____ Him.
3. Define in your own words what it means to "bloom where you are planted."

USE IT
1. List four things that would be difficult about following God even if your friends don't.
2. List a couple of benefits that would come from obeying God.
3. Hearing God speak was the ticket that helped Megan serve. Take time today and listen to make sure you are where you are supposed to be. If you are not, get to where He says go. If you are there already, stay. He holds your future.

Chapter 14

Keeping Your Tank Clean

GET IT

I was seventeen years old and late for a date. My car stopped running in the middle of intense traffic. Not good. Knowing nothing about cars, I called all of my nerd friends who lived to get grease under their fingernails. One of them came to my rescue, and after tinkering under the hood for a whole ten seconds he held up a thing he called a filter and said I had water in the fuel tank. He then proceeded to walk off. I was standing there with a filter thingy in my hand, still without a running car. Good friend and smart but poor helper. I needed to know *what to do* now that I had a fuel problem. We all could use more help like that.

When I do tours, I get to pastor some of our nation's leading Christian contemporary bands. When I do, I try to keep that story in the forefront of my mind. When they link up with me to help, I don't want to leave anybody stranded and stuck. *I want to help people move forward.*

Here is an e-mail I sent to some artists to help them keep their tanks clean.

Hey, guys,

Lately I sense God leading me to be an Aaron for you and your band. In Exodus 17:12 it says, "But Moses' hands became heavy; so they took a stone and put it under him, and he sat on it. And Aaron and Hur supported his hands, one on one side, and the other on the other side; and his hands were steady until the going down of the sun." I have a strong desire to hold up your arms in the battle. From time to time I will be sending you e-mails I hope bring you strength in your inner man and to your band. Charles Spurgeon, in his devotional classic *Morning and Evening* once said, "The nearer a man lives to God, the more intensely has he to mourn over his own evil heart; and the more his Master honors him in his service, the more also does the evil of the flesh vex and tease him day by day."

I have found this to be so true. But admitting to its truth is only the first step to overcoming our self-sabotaging habits. Here are three steps to move us over the "evil heart hump."

1. Admit our hearts are evil. Admit the sin that's in it. I have the tendency to justify. I was tired; at least it's not a major sin, etc. We must believe this spiritual point: What's true about the sin is what God says about the sin, not what we want to say about it.

2. Then we must put forth a plan to rid ourselves of this parasite. The biggest step in any plan to overcome sin is to have accountability. Like what we are doing with the accountability for a clean web time. Accountability means you receive *ability* to overcome bad actions knowing you will have to give an *account* for them, hence "account-ability."

3. Finally it is important that we not only acknowledge what God says about the *sin* but also recognize that what God says about the *sinner* is what's true about the sinner. Otherwise, the vexing and the mourning dominate our thoughts, and we get depressed and discouraged. God says nothing can separate us from His love! God says we can do all things through Jesus. Therefore we can win over sin! When we look in the mirror, we must believe that, although we fail, these encouraging words are true about the evil-hearted person we see reflected.

May the Lord Jesus be with you as you draw closer still and as He honors your service to Him.

CAP IT
1. Who were the two people who helped Moses keep his hands lifted?
2. What is the biggest step in a plan to overcome sin?
3. We can win over _____!

USE IT
1. Take five minutes and admit to God the things that are sinful in your heart.
2. Write out the things you struggle with and have an accountability partner help you overcome them. E-mail the list, text message the person, or meet face-to-face and talk about the list with him or her. Invite your accountability partner to pray with you about these things and to ask you each week how you are developing in your faith over them.
3. Go through Romans 8. Write out all the things God says He is doing or will do for you. Have your accountability partner help you live in light of each of them.

Chapter 15

Weep No More

GET IT

I have discovered that the more I stop and think about heaven the more faith I have about it. During one of my meditation times, I cooked up a little ditty about a perk of our celestial paradise. I want to share it with you today. I hate tears. It breaks my heart to see them roll across a newborn, a teenage, or a wrinkled cheek. *Heaven will be tearless.* I am not much of a poet, but I wanted to reflect on the absence of tears in heaven. May it fuel your faith.

Cries of pain-filled people
rise from this sin-cursed earth.
Forever we'd be imprisoned
except we've had a brand-new birth.
Oh, this blessed birth—
who can price its worth?
A day is in store
when we will weep no more.
In heaven there is no weeping
for the presence of pain is gone.
Keep faith, hurting believer;
soon darkness will turn to dawn.

Oh, this blessed birth—
who can price its worth?
A day is in store
when we will weep no more!
Memory-haunting failures
every day the Christian gets.
But one day we will be basking
in a shoreless sea of no regrets.
Oh, this blessed birth—
who can price its worth?
A day is in store
when we will weep no more!
Comfort one another with these words.

CAP IT
1. What frees us from sin's prison?
2. Our failures are haunting, but heaven will be a _____
   ___ sea of no _____!

USE IT
1. Take a moment and write out a current heartache or pain that is hurting you.
2. Read Revelation 21:4 and ask God to help you absorb its future reality.
3. List a couple of people who could benefit from this same encouragement.
4. E-mail this little poem to them and comfort them with these words.

Chapter 16

A Precipitation Meditation

GET IT

I recently took a trip with my family to my father-in-law's lake house. It's nestled in the midst of a quaint town in Keystone, Florida. Tiny pink houses with large cascading oak trees are sprinkled across acres and acres of small crystal clear lakes. We swam, fished, and raced jet skis. It was so awesome! The thing about it is that a year ago the area was an ugly, destitute wasteland checkered with dried-up lakes. Nobody enjoyed the place because the little bit of water in the lakes was hot and filled with biting worms. YUCK! Sounds like a place mentioned in the Bible called Hades, huh?

But then it rained, refreshing, invigorating downpours of pure heavenly water! It came in what seemed like hundreds of gallons. It covered, flowed, and filled the dryness. Oh, the joy!

One of the most interesting things I noticed was the harsh trench that connected my father-in-law's lake to another smaller lake. We once walked through that trench. Walls six feet high, teeming with roots flanking the sandy banks. A small trickle of stagnant water lined the middle of the "death canyon." If you could get over the creepiness of it all and the smell of something dead (Sponge Bob?), it was sort of fun to walk through. But who wants to walk in a place where you could otherwise be swimming?

I went to check out that spot. Amazing! You could not even see where it once was. The rain had come. The trench was still there, but now it was beneath gallons of sparkling fresh water. I actually drove across it with the jet ski. As I slowly moved forward, I could see to the bottom, and the place that was once an awful journey to endure was an awe-inspiring, breathtaking, fun-filled passage of joy!

Life is like that, with stagnant seasons of struggles. Our spirits get dried up, and we endure the journey. Yes, we love Jesus, but it's life we get upset with. This side of heaven, we will have those kinds of moments. But God will send the rain! Refreshing!

On the horizon, clouds are gathering, and the winds of change are blowing. A downpour is coming! God is going to cover the land with the water of worship, the rain of revival, and the showers of salvation. Get ready to be refreshed. Have faith to believe it. Run to your windows and peer through the shades, eyes to the sky. Keep looking. It's coming!

CAP IT

1. What made the difference between enjoying the lake and enduring the lake?
2. Sometimes we have to endure the journey, but God's rain can transform things into an awe-inspiring _____ _ _____ _____ _____ passage of _____!

USE IT

1. Read Joel 2:23–27.
2. Write a letter to God expressing how you feel about His coming rain and what it means to you. Keep the letter handy and read it in times of drought.

Chapter 17

Vector Hector

GET IT

Hector Cervantes is really into computers. Yea, he plays guitar for Casting Crowns but more often than not on the tour, I would find him sitting in front of a laptop typing away at the keys like a concert pianist. He draws really well and even did the artwork for the T-shirt of the stick people that resemble the band. It is an awesome drawing and a great T-shirt. He can seriously do some awesome graphics and is a PhotoShop guru.

From him I learned about a format in PhotoShop called vector. The cool thing about vector is that you can do anything to a picture and the image doesn't change. You can make it really small or stretch it out to make it really big. No matter what you do, the image stays crystal clear.

Hector is vector! I have known him for eight years now and have seen him in small roles (computer guy doing the Sunday school flyer) and in large roles (busting out a lead guitar solo at a concert). The picture he displays is always clear—it's all about Jesus!

One day we talked about life. He was dealing with the fact that choosing to follow God is about living with a servant heart and a humble attitude. Not long after that something happened, and Hector had an opportunity to demand that things go his way and play the famous artist card to make it happen, but he didn't. He chose to be humble and let God take care of things. Vector Hector. Stretch him and challenge him, and he does not change. He is a humble man of God who lives to keep the image of Jesus the same as a witness to this lost world.

CAP IT
1. Define in simple terms what a vector-formatted image is.
2. How is Hector like a vector image?

USE IT
1. Identify an area in your life that you are not so "vector" in. When you are stretched you change, or when you are in obscurity you scream for attention.
2. Work on those areas by intentionally applying Christ-like principles in them.
3. Clearly describe in one paragraph how you want to display Jesus to the lost.

Chapter 18

Sweet

GET IT

I want to start today's devotion with a moment of personal confession. I am totally into sweets! My favorite has to be butter pecan ice cream. No, it's M&M flavor. No, it must be Oreos. No, it's . . . You get the point. I love sweets, and I could eat all of them foreverrrrrr!

As I sit here in my chair watching some hummingbirds fight over the succulent sugar in my feeder, I'm thinking we may be kin. These guys are fully crazy about the stuff in the feeder. They dart back and forth at each other fighting over who will get the next chance to stick in their beaks and siphon out the clear yummy gold. Their affinity for sweets is undeniable.

The psalmist said he had the same addiction for God's Word. He said God's Word was sweeter to him than honey or the whole honeycomb for that matter. Here is how he put it in Psalm 19:9–11: "The fear of the LORD is clean, enduring forever; the judgments of the LORD are true and righteous altogether. More to be desired are they than gold, yea, than much fine gold; sweeter also than honey and the honeycomb. Moreover by them your servant is warned, and in keeping them there is great reward."

How cool is that? And He was not saying that about the *promises* or the blessings of God, which I really dig, but the *judgments* of God. Did you see that? He is saying God's Word is so sweet to him that he even loves to drink up the judgments! WOW!

How did this kind of affection develop in his heart? I am no expert. My name is Tony, and I am just a guy. But I can make an observation. The only guy who said this "sweeter than honey" thing was a song dude. He loved writing and singing songs. His writings take up the pages of the biggest book in the Bible, Psalms. There has to be a connection. And I think it is this: *what your heart sings about it brings about.* King David was totally into singing about God's Word, and it produced a clinging to God's Word. That is an insight that will give you might!

CAP IT

1. What was it that was sweeter than honeycomb to King David?
2. Which book is the biggest book of the entire Bible?
3. Fill in the blanks: "What your heart _____ about it _____ about.

USE IT

1. Read Psalm 119.
2. Begin developing a playlist on your MP3 player that has songs on it about the Word. A good resource to help you do this would be David Nasser's book *Glory Revealed.*

Chapter 19

Blamelessly Guilty

GET IT

The title is an oxymoron, right? You can't be blameless yet guilty any more than you can have jumbo shrimp. Keep reading. Perhaps you can, and it just may be something that will fuel your faith.

"I did not do it," mumbled my four-year-old in response to my inquiry about the disappearance of my cookie. I turned to look at Bradly. His eyes gleamed with the innocence found only in the face of angels. He said it again: "It wasn't me." Instantly the celestial aura of purity vanished. Big chunks of cookies poured out of his mouth racing to escape his T-Rex chewing and their fate in the abyss of his stomach. As his tongue lunged out to catch some fugitive crumbs, his sheepish smile was asking, "Do you still love me?" He was busted and wanted to be blameless.

Take a peek through the archives of your memory, and I am sure you will find a few "Bradly moments." We take a bite out of the cookie of disobedience, and before we can wipe the residue of our crime off our lips the sweetness of sin turns sour. We shudder from the chill of our guilty nakedness before God, and deep inside we say, "I know I am not blameless. I am so guilty. Will God still love me?" What do we do in moments like this? How can we move in cadence to God's will when we find ourselves acting like a foolish four-year-old?

A good starting point is to remind ourselves that *what is true about us is what God says about us.* And God says we are blameless. In Colossians 1:22 it says, "in the body of His flesh through death, to present you holy, and blameless and above reproach in His sight."

And in Jude 1:24 we read, "Now to Him who is able to keep you from stumbling, and to present you faultless before the presence of His glory with exceeding joy,"

Do you see it? Sure, we sin and try to wipe off the evidence, only to smear it across our faces. But, dear brothers and sisters, God has declared us BLAMELESS! There is no breach in His love toward us. He lovingly corrects us, wipes the smudges off our faces, and invites us to exchange our dessert of disobedience for His buffet of blessing. Unreal yet eternally true! In light of this act of goodness from God, may it lead us to repentance. *We should let the blamelessness we have before God manifest itself in blamelessness for God.* That's what Paul had in mind when he said in Philippians 2:15, "that you may become blameless and harmless, children of God without fault in the midst of a crooked and perverse generation, among whom you shine as lights in the world."

CAP IT

1. Where does our recovery start when we find ourselves acting like a foolish four-year-old?
2. Define what it means to be blameless.

USE IT

1. Here is a short, meaningful prayer you can say out loud to God. "Dear God, thank You! Today we choose to live in light of Your great love. We who are guilty

yet have been declared blameless respond today with obedience fueled by Your goodness."

Chapter 20

Beautiful Mess!

GET IT

I am standing center stage. I just presented the gospel to a packed arena for the Winter Jam tour. Winter Jam was another tour I did, traveling across thirty-two cities with Steven Curtis Chapman, Jeremy Camp, Sanctus Real, Hawk Nelson, and New Song. A roar of applause from sixteen thousand people is shaking the place like a passing freight train. They are celebrating a supernatural God-moment. More than two thousand people have just stood in an act of humility, confessing they have sinful hearts and are surrendering their lives to Christ Jesus as Lord.

My attention is on the faces of those standing. They're a collage of young and old, tattoos and toupees, pierced noses and wrinkled cheeks. I can't keep my eyes off a senior adult hugging a punk rocker. He is weeping. No, it's more like an emotional mixture of laughing and sobbing. His tears have transformed the cool dark mascara-colored circles around his eyes, and he now looks more like a raccoon than a rocker! *It's a beautiful mess!*

I don't want to forget this moment. So with my eyes I swallow an enormous panoramic of the crowd. Then something jumps out at me. Everybody in the place is smiling!

And why not? Two thousand people just connected with what the whole world is looking for, forgiveness and deliverance from the bondage and penalty of sin. Even though I have preached the message more than a hundred times in these arenas, I can't hold back the tears. I am overjoyed, and it's God-joy!

Suddenly the place is vibrating the way my car mirror does when a lowrider hip-hop car rolls up beside me at a stoplight with its subwoofer pounding out a fresh beat! I can't definitively state what's happening, but it's as if all of heaven has joined in the moment. The rush is amazing as we are caught up in a spiritual celebration of wonder and joy. Prophecy is being fulfilled, and Jesus is saving people from their sins! Sinners are now saints, and the beggar in spirit has found a feast of grace and mercy!

The blinking countdown stage clock interrupts the moment and reminds me my time is up and I have to exit the platform. Tears blur my vision as I navigate my way to the stairs around guitar amps and speaker cords. Once I find the floor I hit my knees and bow to the king of glory, and I praise Him for being the God of salvation. May we never lose the wonder of it all!

CAP IT
1. What did I say was a beautiful mess?
2. Fill in the blanks. Sinners are now _____, and the _ _____ in spirit has found a _____ of _____ and _____.

USE IT
1. Get your Bible and find the verse that says Jesus will "save his people from their sin."
2. Write that verse out on a piece of paper, and tape it to your bathroom mirror. Each morning ask God to use you in the process of that prophecy being fulfilled.

Chapter 21

The Devoted DeVevos

GET IT

I love every member of Casting Crowns. They all have such great and unique perspectives and insights. Juan, guitar dude who stands to your right at the concert, and Melodee, fire-breathing violinist and wife of Juan, are no exception. Melodee is quite the boxer chick. I got four bruises from her in the first three weeks of the tour. She just hits you when she is laughing. Juan, who gets hit the most, is so laid back. It seems as if nothing ever startles him, even her punches. The DeVevos are a cool couple, and they both really love and worship Jesus!

Sometime during the tour they got pregnant. We were all so excited for them. Megan who was pregnant at the time was thrilled because now she had someone to enjoy the journey with. But, as sometimes happens in life, joy turned into sorrow. They had a miscarriage. We were so bummed. I hurt deeply for them because I know how much joy a child brings to a marriage. They appropriately kept things very private.

I didn't see them for a long time because we took a Christmas break. The next time I saw them was at a winter conference in Gatlinburg, Tennessee. That's when I put my foot in my mouth. Up till this moment, I did not know that they loss the baby. When I saw them I asked, "Hey, when are you due?" Have you ever tasted foot? I had both of my feet in my mouth! I was so embarrassed and felt so bad for saying something that would bring hurt to their hearts.

But Melodee just looked at me and said, "You haven't heard? We miscarried."

I said I was so sorry.

"Tony, it's ok," she said. "You didn't know."

I drove home that night with a wrench in my heart. I felt so bad. The next time I saw them, I didn't bring it up and instead just watched the two of them. As their band pastor, I thought I would wait till the right moment to bring their loss up again and try to console them. But as I watched them pray together, walk together, sit together, and play together, it was so amazing to see that God was their comfort.

Finally Juan and I had a brief discussion one night before devotions. "Bro," I told him, "my faith is stronger after watching you and Melodee go through such a tragedy yet stay so in love with Jesus and still excited about serving Him."

Juan looked at me and said, "Maybe that's one of the many reasons why God allowed it to happen."

I led devotions that night with a real awareness that Juan and Melodee have shared with us, through their lives, what it really means to be *devoted*!

After I wrote this chapter, I gave Melodee and Juan a copy of what I was going to say to get their approval for the book. What Melodee wrote back revealed again just how much they love Jesus.

I think it is wonderful. We do not deserve to have such things said about us. I don't know if it makes a difference for your book, but we got pregnant at the end of the tour also and had another miscarriage in

May. So it was two in five months. I found out the day after Mother's Day that I was having another miscarriage. This one I took a little better because I knew it could happen again. But in any case I just think that God wants me to think and be more prepared for motherhood than most, and you know when we do have one, he or she will be the most loved kid in the world. I love you guys. Melodee

All the while they stayed devoted to the Lord and played and sang their hearts out each night at more than eighty-seven arenas around America. That is true devotion. God has certainly blessed them for it. As a matter of fact they got pregnant again, and God gave them an awesome little boy. He has the coolest little face and an awesome name—they call him Jesse Dean and he is one of the most loved kids in the world.

CAP IT
1. What were the things I noticed the DeVevos did together after the first miscarriage that inspired my faith?
2. What was Juan's response to my comments of how they inspired me?

USE IT
1. If you are currently going through a trial, read through this chapter again and underline the things the DeVevos did to help each other through it. Merge these practices into your trial.
2. You may not be able to see why God is allowing you to go through a storm, but be certain He is with you all the way. I often listen to the song "Praise You in This Storm" by Casting Crowns, and it helps me hold on. Get it and listen as well.

Chapter 22

Threat Level Low

GET IT

I hate terrorism! I totally can't stand it for a number of reasons: bombings, airplanes into buildings, beheadings, and color changes. Did the color-change thing throw you off? It does most people. They don't see the connection between colors and terrorism. I am referring to the security alert levels our Department of Homeland Security has put together. They go from "green level low," *informing us there's not a phat chance of an attack* to "red level severe" indicating *an attack is imminent.*

I am in the airport every week, and the whole "we are at war" thing is very real there. You go through metal detectors and security officer checks. Currently you cannot even take a bottle of water on a plane because they think it could be a bomb. At the time I am writing this book our level is at "orange elevated." It's serious, and it has taken a certain level of our freedom away.

There is a spiritual terrorist who has his sights set on taking away our spiritual freedom. Doubt, like an insurgent homicide bomber in Iraq, seeks to destroy our faith. Every day doubt explodes in the crowded market of our hearts and attempts to get us to question God and trade in our faith for fear.

To help fight off this terrorist against trust, ask the following question: Once detonated, can the shrapnel of doubt obliterate our Lord's faithfulness? Take a moment and browse through the memory files on the hard drive of your heart. Click on the icons of these past experiences, and we will notice there are no scenes where our God has ever left us. We may have maddening midnights, but His love still illuminates our way; we have faced mighty giants, and yet they tumbled by the rock of God's power flung through the small sling of our weakness!

There is no adversity we have endured that God has not used to make us stronger. Charles Spurgeon once said, "He who has been with us in six troubles will not forsake us in the seventh." Let *the evidence of God's faithfulness* lower the enemy's threat level. Don't go into hiding. Choose to go about your normal activities for God. Through the cross, the threat has been disarmed. Our spiritual security alert level has been reduced to green level low. Proceed in your spiritual journey with joy!

CAP IT
1. What is the name of the terrorist that seeks to destroy our faith?
2. Can the shrapnel of doubt obliterate our Lord's faithfulness?

USE IT
1. Take a moment and browse through your memory files. Write down some of the moments when you have experienced God's presence in your troubles.
2. Get several small Post-it notes and color a large green circle in the middle of them. Stick them all over the place. When you see them, let them fuel your faith

knowing God is with you and will protect you from the devil's attacks.

Chapter 23

Insurrection Injection

GET IT

"Brethren, I do not count myself to have apprehended; but one thing *I do,* forgetting those things which are behind and reaching forward to those things which are ahead, I press toward the goal for the prize of the upward call of God in Christ Jesus" (Philippians 3:13–14, italics added).

Paul was a man on a mission. His faith fueled him toward God-glorifying goals. There is a movement among believers in our nation to be like Paul. I see it everywhere. I am seeing thousands of people standing up for Christ in a world that presses them down. They are leading an *insurrection* whose core purpose is to stop living for the short-lived, insignificant, trivial pleasures of this world but instead exists to advance God's kingdom for His glory.

I recently read a note a teenager wrote to one of his friends. I want to inject it into your minds right now. It personifies this movement. Don't just read it; marinate in its passion.

This is the beginning of a new day. God has given me this day to use as I will. I can waste it or use it for good, but what I do today is important because I am exchanging a day of my life for it. When tomorrow comes, this day will be gone forever, leaving in its place something I have traded for it. I want it to be gain and not loss, good and not evil, success and not failure, so that I shall not regret the price I have paid for it.

What you just read should be the heart cry of every faith-full follower of Jesus Christ. I often read this, and it helps me to stay on target with my God-given purpose in life.

CAP IT
1. What was Paul's mission?
2. What is the core purpose of the current insurrection sweeping our nation?

USE IT
1. Review the last three months of your life. What have they been about?
2. Write out this statement on a card or with a dry-erase marker on your mirror so you see it each morning and let it be a guide for your hearts.

Chapter 24

Rescue

GET IT

The Bible says in Romans 10:13, "Whoever calls on the name of the LORD will be saved." But what does it mean to call on the name of the Lord?

Nine-11, the day lives forever. I wish I could erase the videos of the images that play in the blockbuster of my mind. The images of the planes heading toward the buildings, the fireballs, the people jumping for their lives and buildings crashing to the ground are in my long-term memory. They are horrible.

But good images also came from that horrible day. Images of *people being rescued*! What a joy it was to hear a Fox News alert break in and report about another person pulled from the carnage. There are many heart-lifting stories of people whose lives were saved by heroic rescuers.

As I look back at those people who were rescued, I notice they all have something in common. It's how they responded to the rescuer. Picture the people in your mind's eye. Do you see them there crouched in the midst of suffocating smoke, twisted steel, licking flames, and arching electricity? They are desperately clinging to what might be their last breath. Any moment their lives could be over, but then through the dark smoke they see the light from the helmet of a rescuer. They cry, "Over here! I'm over here!"

Once the rescuer arrives he says, "Sir, you have a gaping wound—you're going to bleed to death." I never heard of anyone trapped blowing it off and saying, "Whatever. It's just a flesh wound." The rescuer might say, "Your neck is broken—don't move a muscle." No one ever shook his or her head around, saying, "Dude, you don't know what you're talking about. My neck is fine." Or the rescuer may say, "Grab me—hold on tight. I know the way out—follow me." No one ever said, "Yeah, right, Mr. Rescuer. I don't need your help. Follow *me*—I know the way out."

No, all of those who were rescued had this one thing in common: *When the rescuer showed up, there was no negotiating!* The trapped people all responded with an attitude of "whatever you tell me to do, I will do it!" "You need to fix my cut? Go right ahead. I need to be still? Is this still enough? Hold on and follow you? You bet. I will do whatever you say! Oh, I'm so sorry I'm cutting off the circulation in your arm, Mr. Rescuer. It's just that if it were not for you I would die. I am completely dependent on you and your ability to help me." And those people who responded that way were rescued. No negotiation with the rescuer, total cooperation and obedience!

Evangelist Bill Stafford once preached that there are three aspects to our salvation. We are saved (salvation), we are being saved (sanctification), and we will one day be saved (glorification). I have come to learn in my experience with Jesus that the way we came to Jesus is the same way we are to continue with Jesus. We came without negotiating, and we continue with Him without negotiation. The believer is to be in a perpetual state of abandonment to Jesus. This is our hope through our passage across this sinful world. And we have this assurance in John 16:33, "In the world you will have tribulation; but be of good cheer, I have *overcome* the world" (italics added).

CAP IT

1. What did all those who were rescued have in common?
2. We are to give the rescuer our total _____ and _____.
3. The way we _____ to Jesus is the way we are to _____ with Jesus.

USE IT

1. List a couple of ways you often find yourself negotiating with Jesus.
2. Read Romans 8:28. Now write it down inside the cover of your Bible. Take time to read it when you are in need of rescue, and it will help you to hold on to Jesus and let Him lead you.

Chapter 25

Big Guy with a Bigger Heart

GET IT

Andy Williams is a big guy with an even bigger heart! Andy is the crazy drummer for Casting Crowns. Everybody may or may not love Raymond, but I know everybody loves Andy!

I will never forget the first time I met Andy Williams. Mark asked me to come up and preach a weeklong meeting for the kids at a Christian school. Mark and the band did the music, and I got to share the Word. We had more than 144 kids get saved the first two days. When the headmaster announced this before the packed auditorium, I heard a loud "OH, MY GOSH!"

It was my first exposure to "Andy the Bald Wonder." We hit it off well. He loved to see God move in supernatural ways, and I loved him for loving that. Andy's spiritual gift is clowning around. He would wrestle with the other guys and go nuts during our Frisbee-golf sessions. During a snowstorm up north, he took off his shirt, and with only a pair of shorts on he went outside and made snow angels! He may be off a little mentally. If you watched the "Andy Show" on the *Lifesong* DVD, then you know what I mean. But Andy holds nothing back! He gets jazzed, and he stays that way.

The coolest thing to me about Andy, though, is that he wants everything about himself to be Andy full of Jesus. He is not a copycat Christian. He's not about pretending. There is no religious junk in his life. It's just one-hundred-percent Andy full of one-hundred-percent Jesus!

His "hold-nothing-back-ness" was always so refreshing. Many times after I preached, I would walk off the stage and see Andy weeping his heart out in praise to God for moving so strongly during the invitation. He had his heart laid out bare and in raw emotion was connecting with our great God. That's Andy, and I love him for it.

CAP IT
1. What was one of the things Andy loved to see God do?
2. What did I say was the coolest thing about Andy?

USE IT
1. List two of the biggest hindrances that try to hold you back from being wide open with Jesus.
2. Understanding you are a unique work of art made by God for God is your ticket to freedom. So revisit the chapter titled Clarity and meditate on it again.

Chapter 26

You've Been Reading My Mail

GET IT

Okay, so you have not read my mail, but you are about to. I have made reference to the Lifesong tour several times. The reason is because it was such a large God-thing. It was one of the most well-attended and spiritually rich concert tours in the world. As we toured, we received tons of e-mail from people who wanted to express their thoughts about our faith being presented at the concert. I thought you might want to take a peek in our inbox and see what a few of them were saying. Their insights and expressions are, let's say, faith fueling.

Texas

I've loved CC's music for a long time. But this concert far exceeded anything I expected and was much more than the music. It was a gathering in Christ's name. Tony Nolan (of whom I'd never heard) did an outstanding 'mini-benediction' (for lack of a better word). I'll admit I was skeptical at first. I'm usually against 'mass altar calls,' as I see so many kids simply moving forward and raising their hands and professing Christ out of emotional peer pressure. Many may disagree, but I don't think Christ wants us to have a knee-jerk reaction to a speaker's touching words and thus confuse it with the touch of the Spirit. This unfortunately leads to a false sense of salvation in youth without truly having been called by the Spirit. I would venture to say this is perhaps better than nothing, but I fear it can result in devastating effects later. Accepting Christ is far greater than an emotional reaction. That said, Mr. Nolan pulled it off flawlessly. He kept it as confidential as possible, thereby lessening the peer pressure effect. Then he set the mood of the house in such a way that the Holy Spirit truly spoke to people, and then Mr. Nolan quite flatly and briefly explained the simple plan of salvation. Well done.

New Jersey

Tony Nolan's time on stage was gloves-off. He said things about our faith that we are sometimes afraid to say to the unchurched. He just set the mood. The Holy Spirit did the work. On the other board I actually received a (message) from Tony Nolan thanking me for my comments but also acknowledging he is concerned about "knee-jerk" reactions himself. The fact that he knows it can happen, will hopefully make him pray specifically about that before he goes on stage. He seems to have his stuff together, so I'll bet he does. Too many preachers/leaders fall victim to the sin of pride when they lead large groups of people. Every Christian leader should be keenly aware of this trap and pray for protection from it. A sermon outlining the path of salvation done under any other influence than God himself, no matter how eloquent or charismatic the speaker, will result in devastation to many lives.

California

I was initially skeptical since I'm against emotional sermons resulting in emotional decisions. The fact is, no human on this earth "saves" anyone's soul. Only Christ can do that. What happened that night is that Casting Crowns and Tony Nolan set the mood and then spoke the truth (in their own gifted ways). Then, in the truest sense of the phrase, something magical happened. I was moved but not so much emotionally. Rather it was the moving experience that only the Holy Spirit, the Comforter, can provide. It was the overwhelming and simple voice of truth.

Here is one that really touched my heart. I have changed all the names to grant privacy.

Iowa

Dear Tony,

My name is Cindy Rains. I am sixteen years old. I live in Hampton, Iowa. I've grown up in a Christian home my entire life, but God wasn't something we talked about daily. Therefore by the time I was in the ninth grade, I believed in God, but I didn't understand that I had much to learn about Him and how to live my life for Him. You see, during ninth grade my life started getting pretty bad. My best friend moved away, my other best friend went to college, and then another best friend of mine died. From about the time school started in September to December, I was bulimic, cutting myself, and pretty much just wanting to die, but not even my family noticed. The first week of December 2005, I attended my best friend's funeral, and that night I attended a Casting Crowns concert at McElroy Auditorium in Cedar Falls, Iowa. You spoke at that concert about having a

Life Lift. Now I was born with a heart condition, and I've had two open-heart surgeries in my lifetime, so I followed every word you said. When I got home that night, I cried myself to sleep because I felt so awful about all the things I had done. Realizing God was there and I needed to give my entire life to Him was the first step to my recovery. So I'm writing to tell you thank you for everything you did for me and to let you know I've never been so close to God in my life, and I'm really glad I am.

Cindy is why we as the church need to be in touch with those hurting people around us. Slow down a little today and listen for their cries and be prepared to watch God use you in amazing ways.

CAP IT
1. Define a knee-jerk reaction.
2. Looks like Cindy had a heart reaction to the experience. She said she felt so _____ about the things (sin) she had done.
3. How much of her life did she say she gave to God that night after the concert?

USE IT
1. Many people think the gospel is bad news so therefore we should not share it. Write the name "Cindy" on a 3 x 5 card. Put it on your refrigerator, and when you go to fill up with something refreshing, remember that, when you share Jesus, people like Cindy with cold hearts can be transformed.
2. Have you shared the gospel with the "Cindys" you know yet? Make time to do it today.

Chapter 27

Peek into My Prayer Closet

GET IT

Today as you enter into your prayer time, I want to give you a backstage pass into mine. I have a prayer book I use every morning. It is filled with strategic prayer lists to help me stay focused.

One of the lists is for my family. They are laser-focused strategic requests I ask God to grant on their behalf. As I have shared these with people around the country, the response has been tremendous. Single people like it because it helps them to know how to pray for their families when they get married. Students like it to pray for their "top five" friends and their current family of brothers and sisters. Moms and Dads use it and begin praying for their kids as never before. Check it out. I know it will be a great source for you to use and fuel your faith in prayer.

Dear Lord Jesus,
  *At an early age may my children come to know
    Jesus as Savior and Lord.
  *Enable us to hate sin and love righteousness.
  *Help us respond to Your chastening with humility,
    brokenness, and repentance.

*Protect us from evil in all emotional, physical, mental, spiritual, and sexual realms.

*Strengthen our submissiveness to You and help us resist the evil one in all things.

*Empower us to be single hearted, focused, and sold out to Jesus.

*Grant our children supernatural wisdom and responsibility in all their relationships.

*Protect our children from harmful associations.

*Endow our children with respect for those in authority.

*Help our children know their gifts, develop them, and serve You in Your church.

*Lead our children to a mate who pleases You, and may Psalm 34:3 be their hearts' passion.

*Fortify our children/mates to be emotionally, mentally, sexually, and spiritually pure.

*Guard my family, and may we be hedged in and protected in all things.

CAP IT

1. I asked God to help us to _____ sin and _____ ___ righteousness.
2. I asked God to help us to be single _____ and sold _____ to Jesus!

USE IT

1. Look at all the prayer requests. Except for the first one (at an early age), list the first word that starts each request.
2. Now using only the first word to each prayer request, say the list out loud. They are all actions. Prayer is evoking God's activity in our lives.

3. Take the time to type up this list on your computer. Then print out a copy of it. I taped mine into the cover of my prayer journal. You may want to do the same and use this list.

Chapter 28

Friendship Factor

GET IT

How would you define the word *friend*? When I asked some of the artists I serve to describe a friend, they said: "Someone you can trust without always having to feel you've got to earn that trust. It's just there." "It's someone you feel comfortable around." "It's a person you can just connect with and drive for hours without having to say one word to them, because you are so comfortable you don't feel like you have to keep anything going. It's already going."

Those were great ideas. Check out these ideas I found on the Internet at www.quoteland.com about friends.

The antidote for fifty enemies is one friend.
—Aristotle
A real friend walks in when others walk out. —Walter Wrenwell
A true friend never gets in your way unless you are going down.
—H. Glasgow
A true friend is united in heart no matter how far apart.
—Unknown

Friendship is like money, easier made than kept.
—Samuel Butler
Friendship is always a sweet responsibility, never an opportunity.

—Unknown

The last quote is what John the Baptist was driving at in John 3:29–30 when he said, "He who has the bride is the bridegroom; but the friend of the bridegroom, who stands and hears him, rejoices greatly because of the bridegroom's voice. Therefore this joy of mine is fulfilled. He must increase, but I *must* decrease" (italics added).

How would you rate yourself on a friendship scale? Do you take the responsibility seriously? Have you ever really thought about Jesus as your friend? You should. To live this life abundantly and fully, we need to take on the responsibility of being a friend to Jesus and all that comes with it. You may be wondering what that means. It's just that we need to be the kind of friend who stands up for His interests, His desires, and His affections, and we never see our friendship with Him as merely an opportunity to cash in on His blessings.

Ouch. That may hurt if your relationship with Jesus has been more like a 9-1-1 call when you need help instead of an ongoing, two-way connection. But don't freak out. The good news is you can change that today.

CAP IT
    1. Friendship is always a sweet _____, never an _____!
    2. What does it mean to be a friend of Jesus?

USE IT
    1. Meet with a couple of your friends and together develop your own definition of friendship.

2. This will be tough, but ask them to write down a few suggestions that could help you become a better friend. Remember that the Bible says the wounds of a friend are helpful.

Chapter 29

Wonder Woman with a Bible

GET IT

I have the utmost respect for Mark Hall's wife, Melanie. In this chapter you are about to see a candid look at the heart of this remarkable Christian. She is a mother of three children, and she home schools them. She is a major leader in the youth ministry where she serves beside her husband, and she is the manager of Casting Crowns. Every time I am around her, I am sure she has a cape growing out of the back of her neck. She is like a saved Wonder Woman, armed with Sharpies, a Blackberry, and a Bible! Melanie is a gift to the world from heaven with a passion for Jesus.

We receive hundreds of letters from people who were blessed at the Lifesong concerts. You just read some of those the other day. But sometimes we get very nasty e-mails from people who are critical and less than encouraging. Many of those "bad" e-mails are complaints that Casting Crowns shared the gospel at the concert. It is amazing to hear people in the church who have a real hard time understanding why a band would have a minister preach the gospel at the concert. The truth is, *our faith is under attack*. Satan wants to steal it or at least keep you from giving yours to someone who needs it. That's why I put these stories in this book to help fuel your faith and arm you against his attacks. The following is a response from Melanie Hall to one of those "ugly" e-mails. Get ready to fill up on one-hundred-percent gospel supreme!

My name is Melanie Hall, and I am the wife of Mark Hall, the lead singer of Casting Crowns. I am also one of the managers of the band. We appreciate your willingness to share your concerns. Oftentimes people have things to share but never do. Thank you for being a supporter of our music and for coming to the concert in Kansas City, Missouri. It was definitely a great night for us.

I am sorry that you were offended by the gospel presentation at our show. When we put together this tour, we had more in mind than just putting together a tour that provided entertainment. As Mark always says, "A concert may change your night, but only God can change your life." We desire to use every opportunity available to us to share God's message of salvation with people that need to hear it. At the same time, our concert is also a little lengthy as it is, and we felt that whoever shared the gospel on our stage should be upbeat and funny, able to catch and keep everyone's attention. Although some may consider Tony's humor more targeted toward teenagers, he never fails to reach children, teenagers, and adults alike with the strong message of the gospel that God has placed on his heart. Since the Lifesong tour began in the fall of last year, over forty thousand people have made public decisions for Christ at our concerts as a direct result of the work of God through Tony's message every night. We praise God for that!! That's why we do what we do.

A few nights ago there was a husband and wife, ages sixty-seven and sixty-nine, that both showed no previous religious connections and yet prayed to receive Jesus into their hearts for the first time. And that is why we travel across the country with our families and work two jobs and make all of the sacrifices that go along with it. Christian entertainment alone is a good thing, just not "our" thing. Thank you again for sharing your opinion. And also thank you for listening to ours. I am sorry that your night with us did not turn out as you had planned. If you contact Proper Management, we will be glad to refund to you the cost of your tickets.

Until the Whole World Hears,
Melanie Hall

WOW! Spoken like an authentic biblical Christian and a lady with class. Props out to Mel! You see, when you live out your faith in a raw, undomesticated way, it will cause great tension with those who only want to be entertained in Christianity. As you embrace the call to live by faith, know you will be attacked. But keep pressing on. Don't let anyone stop you. Remember this: you have the opportunity to be involved in the single most significant event that is going to happen in global history. Bigger than the Revolutionary War. It's bigger than the invention of the printing press or the personal computer or any achievement of all the Nobel Peace Prize winners. What could be that big? The materialization of God enthroned forever! Jesus is coming back! He wants to use you and me to advance His kingdom for His glory. That should be the backdrop behind everything we do *until the whole world hears!*

CAP IT

No questions today. Just try to absorb all the truth she spoke.

USE IT

I have only one thing today. Let Melanie's heart raise you up to be an advocate for the good news of the gospel.

Chapter 30

Pour

GET IT

In 2 Peter 1:5 Peter makes a statement that causes my ears to hone in like a starving bat on a juicy bug. He says, "Add to your faith." This statement implies we need to put additives into our faith. If we do, they will cause our faith to expand—much like the fuel additives we can purchase that help our vehicles get more mileage per gallon. For the last three days of our journey in this book, I want to help you pour an additive in your faith tank that will help you get more out of what you have been putting in.

While on tour with Casting Crowns, Nicole Nordeman, and Building 429, we had church services on Sundays. One Sunday I preached a message dealing with a powerful additive. The additive is called *gratitude*. Add gratitude to your faith, and the powerful combination will cause a radical life change.

Oh, and to keep things lively as we deal with the same topic for three days, I put another little additive throughout the devotion. Note the italics punctuated with an asterisk (*). These are journal reflections about things I saw the artists doing and thoughts I had while I was preaching. I thought you might find it kind of cool to see what I saw and hear what I was thinking while I was delivering this sermon. Reading them will be kind of like a reality TV moment—only it's a "reality reading moment." Enjoy! Pop the latch and open your tank. Let's pour it in.

* I am waiting in the dressing room. Everybody is really tired because we are in New York and we all went "touristing," a word we made up to define what a tourist does. Andy comes in and lies on the floor. He belts out a moan mixed with a sigh. Chris and Hector walk in and have coffee. None for me? Where is the love? Mark was early, as were Megan and Melodee. Where is Juan? I need to start. . . .

Nothing excites a preacher more than seeing someone living out his messages. A young pastor who had been preaching a message series on caring for widows was pulling into his driveway. He noticed a little boy who attended his church standing on the front porch of his neighbor's house. She was a widow. He got out of the car and saw the boy was desperately trying to ring the doorbell but was too short to push it. The pastor thought, *My sermons must be getting through! This boy wants to help this widow!* So the pastor walked up on the porch behind the boy, leaned down, and pushed the doorbell for him, then asked, "Now what are we going to do?" The boy smiled and said, "RUN!"

*Everyone laughs really loud. Mark won't stop laughing because he's like a third grader when it comes to hearing a joke. I'm laughing now at Mark. It's hard not to lose it; got to stay focused. . . .

Sometimes my sermons do not get through. But this morning I hope this one does. I hope you get it because the subject has the potential to invigorate our relationship with Christ and influence others for His kingdom. It will fuel your faith.

Let's take a look at Luke 17:11–17. "Now it happened as He went to Jerusalem that He passed through the midst of Samaria and Galilee. Then as He entered a certain village, there met Him ten men who were lepers, who stood afar off. And they lifted up their voices and said, 'Jesus, Master, have mercy on us!' So when He saw them, He said to them, 'Go, show yourselves to the priests.' And so it was that as they went, they were cleansed. And one of them, when he saw that he was healed, returned, and with a loud voice glorified God, and fell down on his face at His feet, giving Him thanks. And he was a Samaritan. So Jesus answered and said, 'Were there not ten cleansed? But where are the nine?'"

The title of my message to us this morning is "Healed But Still Sick!"

Smiles flash across the room. They like the title, and they have this look that says, "I wonder where he is going with this". . . .

Yes, through a miracle, eyes once swollen shut are now wide open, fingerless hands have sprouted fresh new ones, and parched ravished skin has turned perfectly radiant. But they still had something wrong on the inside. Understanding what they were just delivered from may lend an insight to their issue. Let's think about what has just happened to them. Leprosy was a DSL connection to a dial-up death. Lepers would rot to death. Their facial structure would slowly decay, leaving them without a nose and a mouth without lips. Fingers and toes were reduced to insidious nubs. They were Frankensteins of a sort, grotesque, disfigured creatures on the run from the pitchforks and torches of fear-filled citizens.

All the girls are making faces like they are totally grossed out. Mel is waving her hand in a forward circle motion. I think she is about to hurl and wants me to fast-forward this part. I continue. . . .

Banished to survive on the outskirts of civilization, they would hear the laughs and cheers of the fortunate and rot on the inside as well. Painfully and slowly they would emotionally fall apart, doomed never to receive a hug from their children, have lunch with a friend, or ever hold their lover again.

* Megan's face is covered with compassion; she is a very warmhearted spirit and hurts when others hurt. I wish the world had more Megans. . . .

But one day everything changed. A hideous face transformed to beautiful. A wedding ring found its rightful place again. Stumbling feet regained their strength and raced to deliver a smothering hug to a dear missed child.

*They are clapping and smiling like people do in a movie when the hero saves the day. . . .

CAP IT
1. What was the title of my message?
2. What would make a leper rot on the inside as much as on the outside?
3. What caused everything to change?

USE IT
1. Rent the movie *Jesus* as told from the Gospel of Matthew. As you watch it, write down all the times Jesus saves the day for some hurting person.
2. Describe a couple of ways Jesus has been a hero for you.

Chapter 31

Tilt

GET IT

When you pour something into your gas tank, usually it helps to tilt the container up so you can keep the precious additive flowing. Today is a tilt of the message we started yesterday. Take a moment and reread the story of the lepers in Luke 17:11–17. After you do, pick back up here.

As I continue my message, nobody looks grossed out anymore. Their smiles are beaming! Everybody loves a hero. . . .

This escape from the lepers' asylum comes thanks to Jesus. But as the story reveals, not everyone who should be thanking Jesus is thanking Jesus.

What a predicament to be healed but still sick. Yes, as I said, through a miracle eyes once swollen shut are now wide open, fingerless hands have sprouted fresh new ones, and parched ravished skin has turned perfectly radiant. But *their hearts are still messed up*! They are healed but still sick with ingratitude.

I read a comment on www.quoteland.com from Benjamin Franklin. "Gratitude is the memory of the heart." Well, if that is the case, then these nine lepers were in need of heart surgery to remove the blockage in their memory artery.

*Andy the drummer screams out a big AMEN! I think everybody gets the metaphor, and it resonates. . . .

It is much debated as to whether leprosy is contagious or not. We don't know if these lepers infected anyone with their disease, but what they had wrong with their hearts is definitely widespread! Ingratitude.

I heard that last year *The New York Times* did a piece on "Letters to Santa." Thousands of letters were submitted before Christmas. After Christmas they did another story for people to submit thank-you letters. Only one was submitted. Perhaps Aristotle was correct when he said, "What soon grows old? Gratitude."

Someone has said that gratitude is becoming so scarce these days it can only be found in the dictionary. It's not that bad yet. For the most part, though, our culture breeds ingratitude, and there is an epidemic of this condition.

We should be glad we are not living among the Lilliputians. They were the little people in the story *Gulliver's Travels*. They thought ungrateful people should be killed. They reasoned that whoever makes ill return to someone who blesses them must be a common enemy to the rest of mankind from whom he has received no blessing. And therefore he is not fit to live. Though severe, the reasoning is sound. If a man does ill to one who has helped him, how much more will he do to those who have not helped him in any way? We can thank God that His response to the ingratitude of the lepers and us is not that of the Lilliputians' law. Good news: *God does not want to kill us; He wants to cure us.*

Chris and Hector gesture to each other and sip their coffee together as if they were raising a toast to Jesus, the God of grace and mercy. . . .

CAP IT
1. What was the sickness in the hearts of the nine lepers?
2. How many thank-you letters to Santa were submitted to *The New York Times?*
3. In what way is God different from the Lilliputians about our ingratitude?

USE IT
1. Read Psalm 103:8–11.
2. Write out in your own words how God responds to our sinful ingratitude.
3. Write God a thank-You note.

Chapter 32

Shake

GET IT

When you pay a lot for an additive, you want to make sure you get it all in. So you don't just tilt the container; you shake it to ensure you get every last drop. Today is our last devotion. We've been filling up; you have paid a lot in time and energy. Now let's shake out the last drop of the gratitude additive and get it in our tanks.

*Each countenance is a bit more serious now; listeners seem to be doing inventory in their own hearts, looking for traces of gratitude expressed. . . .

As you recall, nine lepers who had been cured of the awful disease were still sick. They had a heart problem of ingratitude. We can be like that, and when we are, life begins to get really sad and dark. Is there any cure for it? Yes! Ingratitude is curable. Even in the worst of times, we can find something to be grateful about.

I heard a story about Dr. Alexander Whyte who was famous for his pulpit prayers. He always found something to thank God for, even in bad times. One stormy morning a member of his congregation thought, "The preacher will

119

have nothing to thank God for on a wretched morning like this." But Dr. Whyte began his prayer, "We thank Thee, O God, that it is not always like this."

* The band is cracking up. Mark says, "Nice!"

Here are a couple of thoughts from God's Word about gratitude that could help bring us a remedy.

In Proverbs 25:14 we read, "Whoever falsely boasts of giving is like clouds and wind without rain." We have all said we are grateful, but it has to go further than mere words. It has been said that "passive gratitude isn't much use to anyone." Don't just say you are grateful; show your gratitude.

*They are all tracking with me, and they look like they know what I am about to say before I even say it at this point. Mark has that look in his eye that tells me he is going to steal this message. If you hear him preach it, just pretend he wrote it, because everybody knows I wrote the song "Who Am I", yea right. . . .

The phrase "give thanks" is in the Bible countless times. For instance, in Psalm 97:12 we read, "Rejoice in the LORD, you righteous, and give thanks at the remembrance of His holy name." Note the phrase is *give thanks,* not merely *say thanks*. There is a difference. Giving thanks is the next step in the authentic expression of a grateful person who has said thanks.

There is a Chinese proverb that I got in a cookie that said, "When you drink from the stream, remember the spring."

The Lion Sermon Service at St. Katherine Cree Church in London is an excellent example of giving thanks. It is a special service held every October 14 or 15. Each person who comes gets a special gift and hears a sermon that has been preached for more than 250 years. The sermon tells the story of Sir John Gair, who was shipwrecked 250 years ago off the coast of Africa. Upon reaching land, he was confronted by a lion. As the story goes, a lion came up, smelled about him, and prowled round and round him. He was on his knees in prayer, crying out, "Oh, God, I know you delivered Daniel in the lion's den, and you rescued Paul from a lion. Oh, God, deliver me from this beast." When he opened his eyes the lion was running off toward the jungle. After that experience, he gave a large gift of money to the church and asked them to share it with the community every year as an expression of gratitude to God for blessing his life.

Everybody in the room has a look of inspiration and disbelief on their faces. Their eyes resemble a child watching Tinker Bell flying for the first time across the sky at Disney World to start the fireworks. It is a really cool story. . . .

God has done great things for all of us. We can see, we breathe, we have a heartbeat, we have friends, we have food to eat, we have a significant purpose for living, we have gifts, we are saved, we are joint heirs with Jesus, and we are not going to hell! The one who lives by faith in Jesus will always find creative and extravagant ways to express thanks to Him.

There is a buzz in the room now; they all look like puppies dancing behind a glass door, jumping and yelping because their owner is home and they can't wait to lick his face! Everybody is poised to pounce, the message is ending, and they want to run out and give God a big THANK YOU.

CAP IT
1. Write out Dr. Whyte's prayer.

2. What did Sir John do as an expression of gratitude to God for saving him from the lions?
3. Psalm 97:12 implies that we shouldn't just _____ thanks but _____ thanks.

USE IT

1. Write out three of the top things you have to be grateful for.
2. Serving God in your local church is one of the best ways you and I can show our gratitude. Find a ministry that could use some help and do it for Jesus in light of all He has done for you.
3. In addition to serving in a ministry at church, dream up a creative way you could begin a perpetual expression of your thankfulness. Write out what you could do. Now go pull it off!

Chapter 33

Final Thought

I can't think of a better way to conclude this book on faith fuel than to emphasize doing and not just saying. In James 2:26 we read, "Faith without works is dead." You see, once you are fueled with faith, that faith is alive and propels you on a journey. James also said, in James 2:18, "I will show you my faith by my works." The takeaway is simple really: Let's show the world our faith!

You're fueled, and the gas cap is on. All gauges are clear. Pedal to the floor. Enjoy the journey!

Chapter 34

More Fuel

This is my first book, but others are on the way. While you wait, I do have an abundance of other resources that can help you fill up spiritually. The most requested media are our DVDs. They are live messages I preached at conferences, concerts, and churches. I also have several CD series you will find beneficial. Visit our resource store online at www.tonynolan.org. While you are there, sign up to get in on ALL ACCESS. It's a monthly e-mail that connects you to devotions, MP3 interviews, and videos I do for the artists I serve. It has been a joy caravanning with you on this road trip with Jesus.

Printed in the United States
200086BV00002B/235-2025/A

9 781602 668416